D0295519

A Magic Mouse Guide

World Wide Web

by
Chris Ward-Johnson
and the Magic Mouse

Illustrations & layout by
Laughing Gravy Design

CHERRYTREE BOOKS

Editor's note
Computers and software vary considerably. In this book we present
information that is generally true of all computers and show a variety of
screens. Do not worry if your screen is not the same as the one that
appears in the book.

Acknowledgments
The publishers would like to thank the following for permission to use their
photographs and copyright material:
Alta Vista; Microsoft; Netscape UK Ltd; Yahoo!

A CHERRYTREE BOOK

Designed and produced by A S Publishing.

Illustrations and layout by Gary Dillon & Phil Jolly
at Laughing Gravy Design Limited.

First published 1999 by Cherrytree Press Ltd
327 High St
Slough
Berkshire SL1 1TX

In memory of Jonathan Inglis

Copyright this edition © Evans Brothers Ltd 2001

British Library Cataloguing in Publication Data
Ward-Johnson, Chris
World Wide Web. - (Magic Mouse Guides)
1. World Wide Web - Juvenile Literature
I. Title
004.6'78
ISBN 1-84234-077-8

Printed and bound in Belgium by Proost International Book Production.

All rights reserved. No part of this publication may be reproduced, stored in a
retrieval system, or transmitted in any form or by any means, without the
prior permission in writing of the publisher, nor be otherwise circulated in any
form of binding or cover other than that in which it is published and without a
similar condition including this condition being imposed on the
subsequent purchaser.

Contents

Mouse tips

Don't worry if your screen does not always look exactly like the ones in the book

If there are words you don't understand, look on pages 28-31

Mouse tips

3

World wide web

Simon is doing a project on pandas. His friend Liza is helping him. They are looking up information on the world wide web.

The web is like a giant library full of books. It is like a gallery full of pictures. It is like a radio station and a cinema.

INTERNET
SERVICE
PROVIDER

And they are all in your own home. All the information appears on web pages or websites.

The world wide web is part of the internet. The internet is a giant network of computers all over the world. To use the internet you need a computer, a modem and special software from a company called an internet service provider (ISP). You pay the service provider a fee.

And you need a mouse to help you!

Web browsers

To look at web pages you
need a web browser. This may
already be on your computer or it may be
part of the software program from your
service provider.

Liza has a browser called Netscape Navigator.
She shows Simon how to click on the icon on
the screen to open the browser window.
It shows the Netscape home page.

A home page shows you what else is
on the website you have chosen.
It gives you choices about where to
go next.

Anyone can be on the
world wide web. You can have
your own website with your own
home page.

URLs

The name of the browser appears at the top of the window. Below that is a menu bar and a row of buttons you can click on. They give you lots of choices.

The location box gives you the name of the page you are on. Every page on the web has an address called a URL. A URL is a uniform resource locator.

Netscape:Magic Mouse

Back Forward Reload Home Search Guide Images Print Security Stop

Location: http://www.magic-mouse.co.uk

If you know the address of the website you want you can type it in. Simon types in:

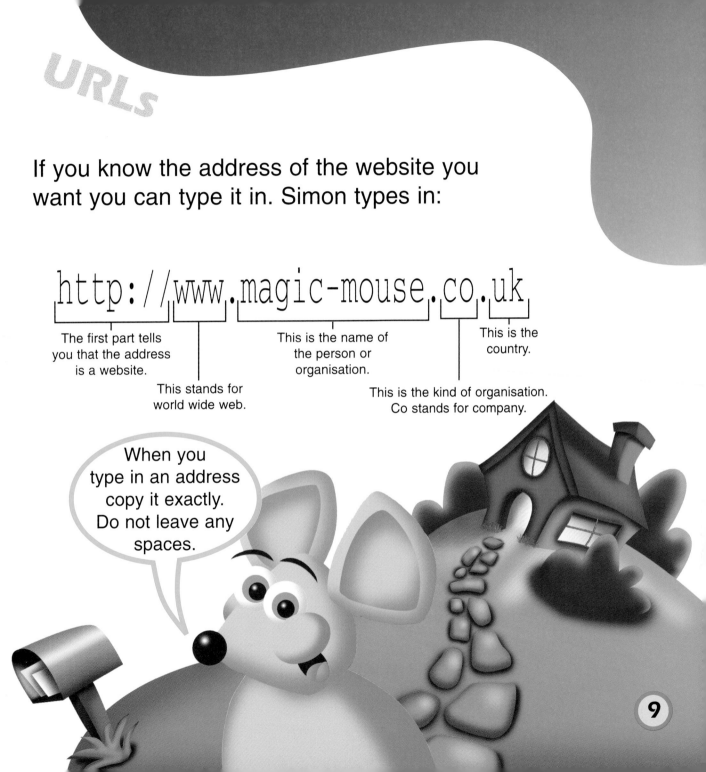

http://www.magic-mouse.co.uk

The first part tells you that the address is a website.

This stands for world wide web.

This is the name of the person or organisation.

This is the kind of organisation. Co stands for company.

This is the country.

When you type in an address copy it exactly. Do not leave any spaces.

Search engines

Simon does not know the address of the websites he wants. Liza shows him how to use a search engine. A search engine lists all the pages on the web. It helps you to browse.

With some search engines you type in keywords. Then the search engine searches for sites that contain the words and gives you a list.

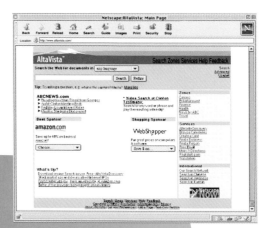

Simon types in 'pandas'. "Help!" he cries.
"There are more than 3000 pages."

Simon tries one and a panda factsheet
downloads on to his screen. It has a
picture of a panda on it. It takes a long
time to appear.

To go quicker
tell your browser not to
download pictures. You
can stop at any time by
pressing the Stop
button.

Hypertext

Simon reads about the pandas and then presses Back to try another choice. Soon he knows a lot about pandas.

Once he starts looking at pages Simon cannot stop. He goes from one page to another. He is surfing the net.

Back Forward Reload Home

Location:

Hypertext

Moving about web pages is easy. They are written in hypertext. Some of the words are in colour with a line under them. When you point at these words a little hand appears. Click on the words and you go to a new page.

The underlined words are called hyperlinks.

Hyperlinks are like magic carpets. They take you to new places.

Menus and bookmarks

Some search engines give you a menu of choices. You select the subject you want from a long list. This leads you to another list and another. Each time you get fewer and fewer choices.

Simon finds out where pandas live, what they eat and why they are in danger. He prints out lots of information.

Back
Forward

Open this link
Add Bookmark for this link
New window with this link
Save this link as...

He puts the best sites in Liza's bookmarks.
Then he can find them easily when he wants
to look at them again. A bookmark is like an
entry in an
address book.

In some programs bookmarks
are called favorites.

15

Saving pages and pictures

Simon looks at all the sites he has chosen. He decides to keep the best one.

He downloads the page on to his computer. Then he selects Save As in the File menu. He answers the questions in the dialog box and saves the page.

But the picture of the panda disappears. What can he do? "Don't worry," says Liza. "Click on the picture with your mouse."

A new menu appears that lets Simon save the picture. He puts it in the same folder as the rest of the page. Now he can print them out when he wants to.

File	
Save	Ctrl+S
Save As...	Ctrl+A
Save As HTML	Ctrl+H

You can look at a saved page without being connected to the internet.

Sounds and moving pictures

Some websites include moving pictures and sounds. Simon wants to hear the noise a panda makes. But Liza's computer does not have a sound card.

Liza's mum lets Simon listen to the sound on her computer. Then he pretends to growl like a panda and chases Liza round the room.

It is best to use headphones to listen to sounds.

HTML

Now Simon has all the information he needs for his panda project. He is going to make a folder to take to school.

"Why don't you use our software to make a panda website instead?" says Liza's mum. "Then your teacher and all the class can see it."

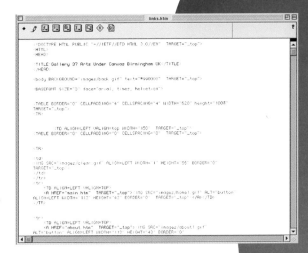

Liza shows Simon how to use HTML. This is a special code that tells your browser how a page should look. It stands for Hypertext Markup Language.

She shows him how to use the program that creates the HTML files. It is like a word processing program and a painting program combined.

Making websites takes time and skill.

21

Making a website

Simon types in his heading: Magic Mouse Panda Project. Then he decides what his topics will be.

Where pandas live. What pandas eat. How to save pandas.

Simon draws up a map showing where pandas live. He scans a picture of bamboo shoots and a picture of some baby pandas. He types in the words of his project.

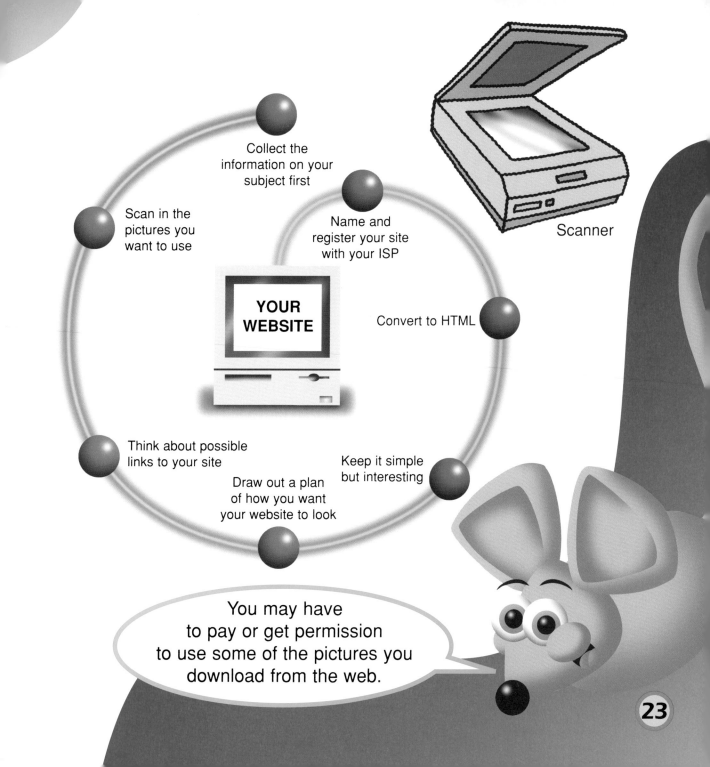

Collect the information on your subject first

Scan in the pictures you want to use

Name and register your site with your ISP

Scanner

YOUR WEBSITE

Convert to HTML

Think about possible links to your site

Keep it simple but interesting

Draw out a plan of how you want your website to look

You may have to pay or get permission to use some of the pictures you download from the web.

23

Publishing your pages

Liza's mum helps Simon to upload his project to their internet service provider's computer. Now Simon's project has its own URL.

Simon's teacher keys in the address and the whole class looks at Simon's project on their screens. They clap and cheer. The teacher gives Simon a software program as a special prize.

Panda Project

After school Simon goes to Liza's house. He gives Liza and her mum a big hug. "Thank you for helping me win the prize," he says.

Why don't you make your own website? You could make one about yourself or about mice.

25

Safe surfing

When you surf the net, you can go to all kinds of sites. You can find out all kinds of information and have lots of fun.

On Netscape Navigator you can press 'What's New' or 'What's Cool' to find new sites. You can find subjects for kids on 'Yahooligans'.

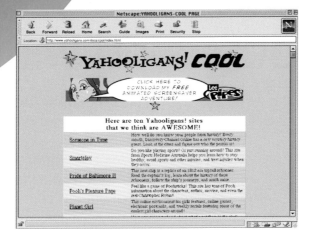

You can download free software. You can read magazines and join newsgroups. You can join mailing lists. You can talk to people in chatrooms.

You can also visit nasty sites by accident, see nasty pictures and meet nasty people.
To stay safe NEVER surf the net without permission. NEVER give your real name and address to anyone. NEVER agree to meet anyone.

Just click your mouse for all the fun of the world wide web.

More about world wide web

Address Every page on the world wide web has its own address or URL.

Bookmarks An address book of your favourite websites.

Browser Software that helps you find your way round the web. Microsoft Internet Explorer and Netscape Navigator are the best known.

Chatroom Channels on the internet where you can 'talk' to other people with the same interests. You need an internet relay chat program to use a chatroom. Ask for permission before you use one and use a nickname, never your real name.

Click Pressing and quickly releasing your mouse. Sometimes you need to double click.

Co This is often part of a web or e-mail address. It stands for company.

Dialog box Window that offers you choices about what you want to do next.

Downloading When a page from the web appears it downloads.

E-mail Electronic mail. A way of sending mail by telephone using your computer.

Favorite Like a bookmark, a way to store a website you often use.

File menu Drop-down list of choices for creating and saving documents

Folder Place where you keep a group of files.

Home page The first page of a browser or website. It usually lists what is on the other pages.

HTML HyperText Markup Language is the language used to make websites. Words underlined in it are links to other web pages or sites.

http Hypertext Transfer Protocol is used to link and transfer hypertext documents.

Hyperlinks Connections between web

pages marked in hypertext by strings of underlined words, often in a different colour.

Hypertext The system that connects all web pages so that you can move from one to another by clicking on hyperlinks or icons.

Icon A picture representing a document, disk or other item on your computer that you can open by clicking.

Internet The worldwide network of millions of linked computers.

Internet service provider A company that you pay to provide a telephone link to the internet.

ISP Short for internet service provider.

Keywords When you type in keywords, your search engine displays a list of sites that contain the words. By combining keywords you can gradually narrow the choice.

Menu A list of commands that gives you a choice of what to do next. Some choices open up dialog boxes.

Modem A device that links a computer to a telephone line and enables the user to gain access to the internet and world wide web.

Netscape Navigator A popular web browser.

Newsgroup A place where you can ask questions or make statements and have discussions on a particular subject. You need special software called a news reader to gain access to a newsgroup. Always get permission to use a newsgroup and never give your real name.

Safety There are some strange people on the internet. Some adults even pretend to be children, so be careful.

- Never tell anyone where you live or where you go to school.

- Never give anyone your phone number or your e-mail address.

- Never give anyone your password.

- Never arrange to meet anyone you do not know already.

- Never meet anyone without asking your parents first.

- If you see or read anything on the web that upsets you, tell your parents or your teacher.

Scanner An electronic device that lets you copy text or pictures on to your computer.

Search engine A site that helps you find other sites on the web using keywords or hyperlinks.

Software A general name for computer programs.

Sound card Part of a computer that lets you play back sounds on your computer.

Surfing Spending time on the internet using hyperlinks to go from one web page to another.

uk Short for United Kingdom, part of most British URLs.

Uniform resource locator The way addresses are written on the internet so that anyone can find them.

Upload To copy programs from your computer on to another computer on the net.

URL Short for Uniform Resource Locator

Web browser Software that helps you find your way round the web.

Web page Any one of billions of documents, or websites, each with its own address on the web.

Website Any one of billions of documents, or web pages, each with its own address.

Window A rectangular area on screen on which documents are displayed for you to read or work on.

www Short for world wide web.

Yahooligans! A search engine set up by Yahoo! that lists pages that will appeal to young people.

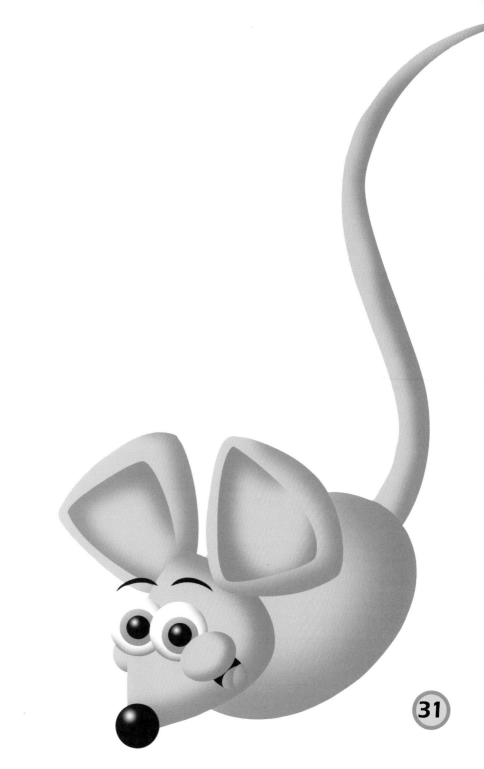

Index